Triumph Over Trials

*Harnessing Job Challenges
into Career Milestones*

Written by
Morgan E. Blake

*Independently published
2024*

Copyright © 2024 by Morgan E. Blake

All rights reserved.

No part of this publication may be reproduced, distributed, or transmitted in any form or by any means, including photocopying, recording, or other electronic or mechanical methods, without the prior written permission of the publisher, except in the case of brief quotations embodied in critical reviews and certain other noncommercial uses permitted by copyright law.

For permission requests, write to the publisher, addressed "Attention: Permissions Coordinator," at the address below.

info@socialized.cloud

Published by Morgan E. Blake

Book Layout ©2024 Morgan E. Blake

Cover Design ©2024 Morgan E. Blake

ISBN: 9798324367275

First Printing, 2024

Introduction: The Journey from Challenge to Triumph

Setting the Stage: What It Means to Triumph in Today's Job Market

In today's rapidly evolving job market, triumph is not merely about landing any position; it's about discovering and seizing opportunities that align seamlessly with one's career aspirations and values. This profound understanding forms the cornerstone of our exploration into what it means to truly succeed in the modern employment landscape.

As we embark on this journey, it's imperative to recognize that the job market of the 21st century bears little resemblance to that of previous decades. The digital revolution, globalization, and the shift towards more fluid, project-based work have all contributed to a new world of work where traditional pathways are being redefined. The dynamics of finding and maintaining employment are more complex than ever, requiring not only adaptability and resilience but also a strategic approach to career planning.

Navigating this new reality demands a clear understanding of one's strengths and the ability

to identify niches where these can be applied most effectively. Whether it's harnessing the power of digital platforms for networking or adapting to new industries that are just beginning to burgeon, success today is about much more than just 'finding a job'. It's about crafting a career path that is resilient to economic fluctuations and rich with opportunities for personal growth and advancement.

In this detailed exploration, we will delve into the essence of what it means to **transform challenges into stepping stones** for career milestones. Each challenge faced in the job market—be it automation, outsourcing, or economic downturns—holds the potential to pivot towards new opportunities if approached with the right mindset and strategies.

The traditional advice of 'keep applying until something comes up' no longer holds water in a world where who you know is often as important as what you know. Thus, modern job seekers must learn to build robust professional networks, leverage social media effectively, and develop personal brands that resonate with potential employers across digital platforms. These skills are not just useful; they are crucial.

Furthermore, the concept of triumph in the job market extends beyond individual successes. It encompasses the ability to contribute meaningfully to one's community and industry, creating value that is recognized and rewarded. This holistic approach to career success is what sets apart the merely employed from the truly triumphant.

By the end of this exploration, readers will have a comprehensive toolkit of strategies and insights that are tailored to navigating the complexities of the modern job market. From identifying emerging job sectors to mastering the art of the digital interview, the insights provided here aim to empower you to not just survive but thrive in your career endeavors.

Through a combination of strategic advice, practical examples, and motivational success stories, this book is designed to guide you through the intricacies of modern employment, helping you build a career that is not only successful but also fulfilling and sustainable. As we unfold the layers of what it means to be truly successful in today's job market, remember that every challenge faced is an opportunity for growth and innovation. Let this book be your compass in the ever-changing landscape of employment, steering you towards a future where career triumph is not just a possibility, but a reality.

Overview of Success Stories to be Explored

As we navigate through **"Triumph Over Trials: Harnessing Job Challenges into Career Milestones,"** it becomes clear that the core of this exploration is not merely about overcoming obstacles, but about understanding and drawing inspiration from those who have already charted paths through turbulent waters. This book dives into a series of **meticulously selected success stories** that exemplify the essence of transformation and resilience in the face of adversity. These narratives not only serve to inspire but also to instruct, offering concrete lessons on turning potential defeats into victories.

The success stories we will explore span various sectors and challenges, reflecting the diversity of the job market and the multitude of obstacles that can arise. From the tech industry's rapid innovations and disruptions to the creative realms where traditional roles are continuously evolving, each story provides a unique lens on how to adapt and thrive.

1. **Tech Innovators:** We'll delve into the journeys of individuals who stood at the brink of technological obsolescence but pivoted to leverage emerging trends. One compelling

narrative includes a software developer who, after a surprising layoff, used his free time to master artificial intelligence programming, subsequently leading to a pioneering role in a groundbreaking startup.

2. **Creative Industry Leaders:** In the realms of art and entertainment, adaptability can often mean the difference between obscurity and fame. Our exploration includes a graphic designer who transitioned into user experience design, capturing the burgeoning demand for digital art skills. Her story is not just about career survival but about thriving by identifying and seizing new opportunities before they became mainstream.

3. **Entrepreneurs:** The entrepreneurial spirit often thrives on challenges, and the stories selected include those who turned personal and economic setbacks into successful business ventures. Consider the story of a restaurant owner whose business was devastated by a natural disaster, yet who transformed his approach to business into a popular food truck, eventually expanding into a new chain of eco-friendly restaurants.

4. **Corporate Warriors:** Those climbing the corporate ladder face their own sets of challenges. We will cover professionals who

have navigated company politics, industry downturns, and personal crises to emerge in leadership positions that redefine their companies' strategies toward more sustainable and employee-friendly practices.

5. **Non-profit Champions:** Success is not only measured in profit but also in impact. Our book highlights individuals in non-profit sectors who have innovated community programs that not only survive but thrive, fundamentally changing the lives of thousands, exemplifying that career achievements are also about creating lasting societal value.

Each story is chosen not only for its inspirational value but also for its educational content, offering readers practical strategies that can be applied to their own career trajectories. These narratives are intertwined with advice on utilizing modern job-hunting tools, enhancing personal branding, and leveraging professional networks in innovative ways.

As we progress through these stories, readers will gain not just a collection of motivating anecdotes but a robust framework for their own career development. These accounts serve as beacons, guiding through the often tumultuous seas of the job market, illuminating paths that others have taken to not just survive but thrive. They reinforce the overarching message of this book: **every challenge encountered is a hidden opportunity waiting to be uncovered.**

By the conclusion of this section, you will have been equipped with the insights and tactics that have propelled others to meaningful and impactful careers. Armed with this knowledge, you are better prepared to craft your own narrative of success, one that echoes the triumphs of those who have transformed trials into celebrated milestones.

Part I: Recognizing Opportunities in Adversity

Chapter 1: Turning Economic Downturns into Career Uplifts

Economic downturns, while daunting, are not just barriers but also bridges to new opportunities if navigated with foresight and strategy. This chapter explores how economic challenges can be transformed into career uplifts, guiding you through the process of identifying and seizing opportunities in times of uncertainty.

The cycle of economic boom and bust is inevitable, yet each downturn carries its unique set of challenges and opportunities. Historically, periods of economic stress have forced industries to evolve, businesses to innovate, and individuals to reassess and realign their career paths. Understanding this cycle is the first step towards turning an economic crisis into a career opportunity.

Identifying Opportunities Amidst Challenges During economic downturns, certain sectors may contract, but others might experience growth or transformation. For instance, the financial crisis of 2008 led to a surge in regulatory jobs within the financial sector, while the digital revolution expanded roles in IT and cybersecurity in response to increased digital transactions and threats. Similarly, the recent global pandemic has drastically changed the landscape, accelerating remote work and boosting industries such as e-commerce, digital marketing, and telehealth.

Strategies for Career Pivoting

Pivoting during a downturn requires a strategic approach:

- **Skill Enhancement:** Upgrading your skills or acquiring new ones relevant to growth industries is crucial. This could mean taking online courses in data analytics, digital marketing, or other areas that are in demand.

- **Networking:** Building and nurturing professional relationships is more crucial than ever. Engage with online networking groups, attend virtual conferences, and connect with industry leaders on platforms like LinkedIn.

- **Flexibility:** Being open to contract work, part-time roles, or different sectors can provide not only a stopgap but also an entry point into new fields. Many successful career transitions begin with a willingness to step into less familiar roles that offer long-term growth potential.

Real-Life Examples of Career Transformation

Consider the story of Maria, who worked in retail management. During the economic downturn, her company downsized, and she lost her job. Instead of seeking another job in retail, Maria leveraged her skills in personnel management and customer service to transition into a customer success role in a tech company. She took short courses in tech support and customer relationship software to make her more marketable in this new industry.

Leveraging Economic Indicators

Understanding economic indicators such as employment rates, industry growth trends, and government economic policies can provide insights into where opportunities might be emerging. Keeping abreast of these indicators enables proactive career planning and positioning.

Staying Motivated and Resilient

Maintaining a positive outlook is essential. Economic downturns can be stressful and disheartening, but resilience and motivation are key to seeing through these periods. Setting short-term goals, celebrating small wins, and maintaining a routine can help sustain momentum.

Conclusion of the Chapter

As we examine the stories and strategies in this chapter, remember that economic downturns, while challenging, are not the end of a career but a complex maze that, with the right mindset and tools, can lead to unexpected and rewarding career paths. This chapter provides a roadmap for navigating these tumultuous times, offering actionable steps to not only survive but thrive and turn economic adversity into a stepping stone for career success.

In essence, the ability to turn economic downturns into career uplifts lies in understanding the evolving landscape, being adaptable, and proactively seeking opportunities to use your skills in new and emerging fields. Let this chapter serve as your guide to transforming economic trials into triumphant career transitions.

Chapter 2: Navigating Career Transitions: From Layoffs to Leadership

Layoffs are often perceived as a professional setback, but with the right perspective and tools, they can be transformed into powerful catalysts for career advancement. In this chapter, we delve into the strategies and mindsets that enable such transformations, turning what seems like an end into a significant new beginning.

Understanding the Psychological Impact of Layoffs

The initial impact of a layoff can be psychologically daunting. It's important to acknowledge the emotions that come with job loss—fear, uncertainty, and doubt. However, processing these emotions is the first step in paving a new path forward. By reframing the experience as an opportunity for growth and exploration, one can begin to navigate the transition with a sense of purpose and direction.

Strategic Steps to Leadership After a Layoff

Transitioning from a layoff to a leadership role involves several strategic steps:

- **Self-Assessment:** Evaluating one's skills, interests, and values is crucial. This self-assessment helps in identifying not just any job, but the right role that aligns with personal and professional goals.

- **Skill Development and Education:** Layoffs can provide the time and motivation needed to upgrade one's skills. Whether it's pursuing an advanced degree or obtaining certifications, enhancing one's qualifications is key to making oneself more marketable and prepared for higher-level positions.

- **Networking:** Reaching out to industry contacts, joining professional groups, and attending seminars are vital actions. Networking isn't just about finding a job; it's about building relationships that can offer support, provide advice, and open doors to opportunities that may not be publicly advertised.

- **Strategic Job Searching:** Instead of a broad approach, a targeted job search focused on specific industries or roles can be more effective. Utilizing job boards, recruitment agencies, and professional networks strategically can yield more pertinent opportunities.

- **Personal Branding:** Articulating one's personal brand through a compelling resume, a robust LinkedIn profile, and a professional online presence is essential. This branding should communicate one's unique skills, experiences, and the value they bring to potential employers.

Real-Life Success Stories

Consider the case of John, a middle-management executive in the automotive industry who was laid off during a restructuring wave. Instead of rushing back into the job market, John evaluated his long-term career desires and realized his passion for sustainability. He pursued a certification in sustainable business practices, which allowed him to transition into the renewable energy sector. Within a year, John secured a leadership role in a firm dedicated to innovative energy solutions, turning his layoff into a stepping stone towards a fulfilling new career path.

Leveraging Leadership Skills

For those aspiring to leadership roles post-layoff, it's critical to demonstrate leadership skills even when not formally in a leadership position. This can be achieved by:

- **Leading Projects:** Volunteering to lead initiatives, even on a small scale, can highlight leadership capabilities.

- **Mentoring:** Offering guidance to peers or less experienced professionals can help develop and showcase leadership qualities.

- **Thought Leadership:** Writing articles, speaking at industry events, or participating in panel discussions can establish one's reputation as a thought leader in the field.

Embracing a Forward-Thinking Mindset

It's essential to adopt a forward-thinking mindset that focuses on future possibilities rather than past setbacks. This mindset, coupled with resilience and proactive planning, can transform a layoff into a launchpad for a more satisfying and impactful career.

As this chapter concludes, remember that navigating career transitions successfully requires more than just finding a new job; it involves a deep transformation of one's approach to work and life. This transformation, guided by strategic thinking and continuous learning, paves the way not just to recovery but to true professional triumph.

Chapter 3: Innovating Job Search Strategies in the Digital Era

The landscape of job searching has undergone a radical transformation in the digital era, reshaping how we connect with potential employers, discover opportunities, and present ourselves professionally. This chapter delves deep into innovative strategies that harness the power of digital tools to navigate the job market more effectively, ensuring that you stand out in an increasingly competitive environment.

The Shift to Digital Platforms

The advent of digital technology has shifted the job search from traditional methods like newspaper ads and walk-in interviews to sophisticated online platforms. Today, job seekers must be adept at navigating a variety of digital channels, from job boards and corporate websites to professional social networking sites like LinkedIn. Understanding these platforms' algorithms can significantly enhance your visibility to potential employers.

Optimizing Your Digital Presence

A robust digital presence is crucial in today's job market. It begins with a professional LinkedIn profile that showcases your skills, experiences, and career accomplishments. But it doesn't stop there:

- **Professional Websites and Portfolios:** For many professionals, particularly in creative and tech fields, a personal website or online portfolio can be a game-changer. These platforms allow you to showcase your work, share your career narrative, and provide a direct contact method for potential employers or collaborators.

- **SEO for Personal Branding:** Understanding and applying SEO (Search Engine Optimization) principles to your online content can dramatically increase your visibility. Use relevant keywords in your LinkedIn profile, blog posts, and professional websites to improve your search rankings and attract more views.

Leveraging Social Media for Job Searching

Social media platforms offer more than just networking opportunities; they are potent tools for job searching. Platforms like Twitter, Instagram, and even Facebook can be used to follow companies, join professional groups, and engage with content relevant to your field, increasing your industry visibility.

- **Twitter:** Follow industry leaders and participate in relevant conversations using hashtags. Twitter chats are often used for professional discussions and can connect you with influencers and hiring managers.
- **Instagram:** Useful for creative fields, Instagram allows you to showcase your work visually and build a follower base interested in your professional capabilities.

Advanced Tools and Analytics

Harnessing advanced tools and analytics can give you an edge in the job search process. Many job boards and websites offer advanced search options that allow you to filter positions by keywords, location, experience level, and more. Additionally, analytics tools can provide insights into the demand for specific roles and the skills required, enabling you to tailor your application materials accordingly.

Networking in the Digital Age

Digital networking has become an essential strategy. Virtual job fairs, webinars, and online workshops provide platforms not only for learning but also for connecting with peers and industry leaders. Effective digital networking involves:

- **Engagement:** Regularly comment on, share, and discuss posts by your connections. This keeps you visible and relevant within your network.
- **Professional Groups and Forums:** Join groups and forums on LinkedIn, Facebook, and niche websites where you can contribute to discussions, share insights, and even discover hidden job opportunities.

Case Studies: Success Through Innovation

Consider the example of Emma, a digital marketer who used targeted LinkedIn ads to showcase her portfolio directly to decision-makers at her dream companies. By creating compelling ad content and selecting precise demographics, she gained interviews and eventually a senior position.

Embracing a Culture of Continuous Learning

The digital era demands that job seekers not only adapt to current technologies but also continuously learn and anticipate future trends. This involves staying updated with new tools, upgrading skills through online courses, and consistently adapting your strategies to the evolving digital landscape.

This exploration equips you with the understanding and tools necessary to master the art of the digital job search. With these strategies, you can navigate the complexities of the modern job market, ensuring that your digital footprint is not just a footprint but a firm step towards your next career milestone.

Part II: Strategic Tools for Modern Job Hunting

Chapter 4: Leveraging Social Media for Career Advancement

In the digital age, social media has transcended its original purpose of social networking to become a pivotal platform for professional growth and career advancement. This chapter explores how to effectively harness the power of social media to enhance your professional visibility, connect with key industry players, and open doors to new career opportunities.

Building a Professional Online Persona

The foundation of using social media for career advancement is to establish a professional online persona that accurately reflects your professional identity and aspirations.

- **Consistency Across Platforms:** Ensure that your LinkedIn, Twitter, Facebook, and any other professional profiles present a coherent professional image. This includes a professional photo, a compelling bio, and uniformity in the way you describe your skills and experiences.

- **Content Sharing:** Regularly share and produce content that is relevant to your field. This could include articles, blog posts, project updates, and insightful commentary on industry trends. This not only demonstrates your engagement and expertise but also keeps you visible in the feeds of your connections and increases the likelihood of your content being shared by others, expanding your reach.

Engaging with Industry Leaders and Peers

Social media offers unprecedented access to industry leaders and peers who might otherwise be out of reach.

- **Follow and Interact:** Follow companies, thought leaders, and influencers in your field. Actively engage with their posts by liking, commenting, and sharing. Thoughtful comments can spark conversations and help you get noticed.

- **Join Professional Groups:** Platforms like LinkedIn and Facebook host numerous professional groups where you can discuss current issues, ask questions, and share insights. Participation in these groups can lead to connections that may prove invaluable in your job search and professional development.

Using Social Media to Research Companies

Social media is a powerful tool for gaining insights into company cultures, upcoming job openings, and news. Follow the social media accounts of target companies to:

- **Learn About Company Culture:** Many companies share posts related to their work environment, corporate events, and team activities. This can give you a clearer picture of their values and what they might be looking for in candidates.

- **Stay Updated on Job Openings:** Companies often announce new openings on social media before they appear on job boards. Following them can give you a head start on applications.

- **Engage with Company Posts:** Commenting on company posts can increase your visibility to the company's HR team. Make sure your comments are professional and insightful.

Crafting a Personal Brand

Social media allows you to build and project a personal brand that can attract potential employers.

- **Define Your Unique Value Proposition:** What do you offer that others don't? Your social media profiles should clearly communicate your unique skills, experiences, and the value you bring to a potential employer.

- **Showcase Your Achievements:** Regularly update your network about your professional achievements, such as completing projects, participating in conferences, or any recognitions you have received. This keeps your network engaged and informed of your capabilities.

Navigating Challenges and Pitfalls

While social media is a powerful tool for career advancement, it also comes with challenges that need to be carefully managed.

- **Maintain Professionalism:** Always be mindful of the content you post and share. Avoid controversial topics and keep your interactions professional, as potential employers often review social media profiles before making hiring decisions.

- **Privacy Settings:** Be aware of your privacy settings and who can see your posts. It's important to manage the visibility of different types of content to appropriate audiences.

Harnessing the Full Spectrum of Social Media Tools

Beyond just networking and job searching, social media platforms offer various tools like hashtags, live videos, and stories, which can be strategically used to enhance your visibility and engagement. For example, Instagram Stories can be used to share moments from professional events or behind-the-scenes glimpses of your work life, adding a personal touch that can make your profile more relatable and engaging.

As we wrap up this detailed exploration, it's clear that when used thoughtfully, social media is not just a tool for connecting with friends but a career-enhancing resource that can significantly impact your professional journey. By adopting the strategies outlined above, you are well-equipped to navigate the complexities of the digital landscape and use social media to forge a path to career success.

Chapter 5: Networking: The Unseen Lifeline of Successful Careers

In the intricate tapestry of career development, networking emerges not merely as a thread but as a vital lifeline, connecting the myriad dots of opportunities and potential pathways. This chapter unravels the profound impact of networking, revealing how it propels careers from the shadows of obscurity to the spotlight of leadership and innovation.

The Essence of Networking

Networking goes beyond collecting business cards and LinkedIn connections; it involves building and nurturing relationships that provide mutual value over time. Effective networking isn't transactional but transformational. It involves:

- **Active Engagement:** Regular interaction with your network, offering assistance, sharing knowledge, and congratulating others on their achievements.

- **Sincerity in Relationships:** Genuine interest in the success of others, which builds trust and fosters a willingness to support each other.

Strategies for Effective Networking

To harness the full potential of networking, one must strategize not only how to build connections but also how to maintain and leverage them effectively:

- **Attending Industry Events:** Conferences, seminars, and workshops are goldmines for meeting new people in your field. The key is not just to attend but to engage—ask questions, participate in discussions, and follow up afterward.

- **Volunteering:** Offering your skills to a professional organization or charity aligns you with others who share similar values and can dramatically broaden your network.

- **Informational Interviews:** These can provide insights into your field or a company you're interested in and establish connections that may later lead to job opportunities.

Digital Networking and Its Impact

In today's digital world, networking extends into the virtual realm, providing tools that can amplify traditional networking methods:

- **Professional Online Platforms:** LinkedIn is the quintessential tool for professional networking, but platforms like Twitter and even Instagram can be leveraged for connecting with industry professionals.

- **Webinars and Virtual Meetups:** These events can offer opportunities to engage with leaders and peers from around the globe without the need for travel.

Leveraging Networks for Career Transitions

Networking can be particularly valuable when you are looking to change careers or industries. It allows you to:

- **Gain Industry Insights:** Conversations with established professionals offer valuable perspectives that can help you navigate your new field.

- **Find Mentors and Sponsors:** These are people who can provide guidance, introduce you to key individuals, and advocate on your behalf.

The Role of Networking in Job Searches

Most jobs are not advertised publicly, and here, networking becomes crucial. It provides a pathway to these hidden opportunities through referrals which often lead to interviews. Moreover, a recommendation from a trusted contact can significantly boost your chances of securing a job.

Networking as a Lifelong Process

The most successful professionals view networking as a lifelong component of their careers. Continuously expanding your network and nurturing existing relationships can lead to opportunities far beyond a job search, including partnerships, mentorships, and collaborative projects.

Building a Diverse and Inclusive Network

In today's global job market, having a diverse network is invaluable. It exposes you to different perspectives and ideas, enhancing your creativity and problem-solving skills. Actively seek to connect with individuals from various backgrounds, industries, and cultures to enrich your professional experience and understanding.

As we close this discussion, remember that networking is about much more than advancing your own career; it's about creating a community of support and opportunity. It involves contributing as much as you gain, forming bonds that can withstand the test of time and career changes. With the strategies laid out in this chapter, you are well-prepared to weave a network that not only supports your current career aspirations but also paves the way for future successes and innovations.

Chapter 6: Mastering Remote Job Interviews and Virtual Hiring Processes

As the professional world embraces the nuances of the digital age, mastering remote job interviews and virtual hiring processes has become an essential skill for job seekers. This chapter provides a detailed guide to navigating this new terrain, ensuring you are equipped to shine in virtual settings and secure your place in the increasingly remote workforce.

Understanding the Virtual Interview Landscape

The first step in excelling at remote interviews is understanding the environment and tools commonly used. Platforms like Zoom, Skype, Microsoft Teams, and Google Meet have become the standard mediums for conducting professional interviews remotely. Familiarity with these technologies is not just beneficial; it is essential.

Preparing for the Virtual Interview

Preparation for a virtual interview should be as thorough as for an in-person meeting, if not more so due to the technical elements involved.

- **Technical Setup:** Ensure your internet connection is stable, your webcam and microphone are of good quality, and the software needed for the interview is installed and up-to-date. Conduct a test run with a friend to troubleshoot potential issues.

- **Environment:** Choose a quiet, well-lit space for the interview. The background should be professional and tidy—neutral walls are preferable, with minimal distractions.

- **Dress Code:** Dress professionally, just as you would for an in-person interview. This not only influences how you are perceived but can also affect your own mindset and performance.

Enhancing Communication Skills for Virtual Formats

Communicating effectively in a virtual format requires specific considerations:

- **Verbal Communication:** Speak clearly and at a moderate pace to ensure your audio is easy to understand. Articulate your responses thoughtfully and use concise language.

- **Non-Verbal Communication:** Maintain good posture and eye contact by looking at the camera, not the screen. Use hand gestures moderately; excessive movement can be distracting on video.

Anticipating and Answering Interview Questions

Anticipating common interview questions and preparing thoughtful responses should be part of your interview preparation. Additionally, be ready to discuss how you manage remote work and use digital tools, as these are often relevant topics in virtual interviews.

- **Behavioral Questions:** Be prepared with examples that demonstrate your ability to manage projects, communicate effectively, and resolve conflicts, especially in remote settings.

- **Technical Questions:** Depending on the job, you may also need to prepare for practical demonstrations or technical discussions. Ensure you understand the tools and methods relevant to your field.

Following Up Post-Interview

A follow-up thank-you email is as crucial after a virtual interview as it is in person. It should be sent within 24 hours of the interview to express gratitude for the opportunity and to reiterate your interest in the position.

Common Pitfalls to Avoid

Several pitfalls can undermine the effectiveness of a virtual interview:

- **Technical Difficulties:** Poor audio quality, a bad connection, or unfamiliarity with the interview platform can disrupt the flow of conversation and cause frustration on both ends.

- **Distractions:** Interruptions from household noises, phone calls, or emails can detract from your professionalism. Ensure you manage your environment to minimize these risks.

- **Over-rehearsing:** While preparation is crucial, over-rehearsing can make your responses come across as insincere or scripted. Aim for a balance that allows you to appear prepared yet natural.

Embracing the Digital Interview Era

The shift to remote interviews can be seen as an opportunity rather than a challenge. It allows for greater flexibility, saves on travel time, and can make the interview process more efficient. By embracing this shift and preparing diligently, you position yourself as a forward-thinking, adaptable candidate, well-suited for the modern workplace.

As we conclude this exploration of remote job interviews and virtual hiring processes, it becomes clear that the digital world offers unique opportunities to demonstrate your professionalism and readiness for the challenges of today's job market. By mastering these digital dynamics, you are not just preparing for an interview; you are preparing for a successful career in an increasingly virtual world.

Part III: Case Studies of Success

Chapter 7: The Career Resilience of Tech Innovators

In the dynamic realm of technology, resilience is not just a trait but a prerequisite for survival and success. This chapter explores the profound resilience of tech innovators who have transformed industry challenges into groundbreaking opportunities, marking their indelible impact on the digital world.

Navigating the Fast-Paced Tech Landscape

The technology sector is characterized by rapid evolution, where today's innovations can become tomorrow's obsolescence. Tech professionals must not only keep pace with swift technological advancements but also anticipate and adapt to these changes proactively. This ability to adapt is often what distinguishes successful innovators in tech.

Case Studies of Resilient Tech Leaders

Drawing from real-life examples, this section delves into the careers of tech leaders who exemplify resilience:

- **Elon Musk:** Known for his work with Tesla and SpaceX, Musk's journey is a testament to turning visionary ideas into reality amidst skepticism and immense technical challenges. His commitment to renewable energy and space exploration has spurred significant technological advancements.

- **Sheryl Sandberg:** As COO of Facebook, Sandberg navigated the company through numerous controversies and growth challenges, emphasizing the importance of leadership and adaptability in maintaining a company's edge in a competitive market.

- **Satya Nadella:** Under Nadella's leadership, Microsoft experienced a renaissance by shifting focus from solely software to cloud computing and technology solutions, demonstrating strategic resilience in adapting business models to market needs.

Building Resilience in Tech Careers

For those looking to forge a resilient career in technology, several strategies are pivotal:

- **Continuous Learning:** Stay abreast of emerging technologies through courses, certifications, and self-directed learning. Platforms like Coursera, Udacity, and Pluralsight offer resources tailored to tech professionals.

- **Innovation Mindset:** Cultivate an environment where innovation is encouraged. This involves taking calculated risks and embracing failures as learning opportunities.

- **Networking within Tech Communities:** Engage with online forums, local meetups, and conferences to connect with other professionals who can provide support, insights, and opportunities in your field.

The Role of Mentorship and Community

Mentorship is particularly valuable in the tech industry. Having a mentor who has navigated the technological and business challenges you face can provide guidance, encouragement, and an invaluable perspective. Furthermore, participating in tech communities, whether online or in-person, can enhance resilience by providing a support network that fosters shared learning and collaboration.

Leveraging Setbacks as Stepping Stones

Many tech innovators have faced setbacks that seemed insurmountable at the time. The key to their resilience has been their ability to use these setbacks as stepping stones. For example, the development of the iPhone was fraught with technical challenges and doubts, yet it became a transformative product that reshaped the mobile industry. The lesson here is clear: resilience involves seeing beyond the immediate hurdles and maintaining a focus on longer-term goals.

Embracing Change and Uncertainty

In technology, change is the only constant. Embracing this reality is crucial for developing resilience. This means being prepared to pivot when necessary, whether this involves shifting your focus to new technologies, adapting to new business models, or even changing roles within the industry.

As this exploration concludes, it becomes evident that resilience in the tech industry is about more than enduring; it's about thriving in the face of adversity. By understanding the journeys of those who have navigated this volatile landscape successfully, you gain not only inspiration but also practical strategies that can fortify your own path to success. This chapter equips you with the tools to not only survive the tech industry's trials but to use them as catalysts for your own innovative contributions.

Chapter 8: Creative Industries: Adapting and Thriving Against the Odds

In the vibrant tapestry of the creative industries, from graphic design to filmmaking, music production to digital media, adaptability is not merely an asset but a necessity. This chapter delves deep into the resilience and adaptability required to navigate the unique challenges faced by professionals in the creative fields, illustrating how they can thrive against the odds.

The Ever-Evolving Creative Landscape

The creative industries are marked by continuous evolution, driven by shifts in cultural trends, technological advancements, and consumer behavior. Success in these fields demands not just talent and skill, but a perpetual readiness to adapt and innovate. Embracing change is often the difference between relevance and obscurity.

Technological Disruption and Opportunity

Technology has radically transformed the creative sectors, altering the way art is produced, marketed, and consumed. Digital platforms have democratized access to audiences but also increased competition. Successful creatives are those who leverage new technologies to enhance their artistry and reach:

- **Digital Art and Design:** Graphic designers and visual artists have moved from traditional media to software like Adobe Creative Suite and platforms like Procreate, expanding their capabilities in digital art.

- **Music and Sound Production:** The shift from analog to digital has transformed how music is produced, mixed, and distributed. Platforms like SoundCloud and Spotify allow musicians to reach global audiences directly.

- **Film and Video Production:** Digital technologies have revolutionized filmmaking, with high-quality equipment becoming more affordable and editing software more accessible, enabling independent filmmakers to produce content that was once the domain of major studios.

Navigating Financial Instability

One of the perennial challenges in the creative industries is financial volatility. Many creative roles are project-based or freelance, leading to periods of financial uncertainty. Thriving in this environment requires not only financial management skills but also strategic planning:

- **Diversification:** Successful creatives often diversify their income streams. A graphic designer might also teach online courses, write blogs about design theory, or sell original artwork.

- **Financial Planning:** Effective budgeting and financial planning are crucial, especially when income is irregular. Many creatives use tools like Mint or You Need a Budget (YNAB) to manage their finances.

Building a Personal Brand

In the crowded marketplace of the creative industries, a strong personal brand can set you apart. This involves:

- **Consistent Messaging:** Your brand should reflect your unique voice and style across all platforms and interactions.

- **Engagement:** Building a loyal following involves regular engagement with your audience through social media, newsletters, and personal interactions.

Case Studies of Creative Resilience

Exploring real-life examples offers valuable insights:

- **An independent filmmaker:** Who used crowdfunding to finance her projects, effectively engaging her audience in the production process and securing the necessary funds to continue her work despite traditional funding barriers.
- **A digital artist:** Whose innovative use of augmented reality in art installations captured the attention of major galleries and led to lucrative collaborations with tech companies.

Adapting to Market Needs

Understanding and anticipating market trends is crucial. This might mean adapting techniques to suit changing tastes or exploring new mediums and technologies to stay ahead of the curve.

The Importance of Community and Collaboration

No creative is an island. The most resilient professionals in the creative industries are often those who actively seek collaboration and support within their communities. Networking, both online and in person, can lead to opportunities, partnerships, and collaborative projects that might not have been possible solo.

As we conclude this examination of the creative industries, remember that the challenges you face—whether technological advancements, financial instability, or intense competition—can be transformed into opportunities to innovate and excel. This chapter not only celebrates the dynamic nature of creative work but also provides practical strategies to ensure that you, as a creative professional, are not just surviving but thriving, turning your unique challenges into stepping stones for success.

Chapter 9: Entrepreneurs and the Art of Turning Setbacks into Start-ups

Entrepreneurship is inherently about charting unknown waters and turning the tides of setbacks into the winds that propel new ventures. This chapter explores the artistry of entrepreneurship, focusing on how challenges and failures are not just obstacles but essential ingredients for innovation and the birth of startups.

Understanding the Entrepreneurial Mindset

The entrepreneurial journey starts with a mindset that views challenges as opportunities. This perspective is crucial because it dictates responses to setbacks—not as signals to retreat but as calls to innovate and pivot.

- **Risk Tolerance:** Entrepreneurs often face significant uncertainties and must be comfortable taking calculated risks. This involves assessing potential losses and having contingencies in place.

- **Persistence and Resilience:** The paths to startup success are fraught with hurdles. The ability to persevere through downturns, learn from failures, and continue moving forward is essential.

- **Vision and Adaptability:** While having a clear vision is vital, the capability to adapt that vision in response to new information, market feedback, and changing circumstances can make the difference between a failing venture and a successful one.

Turning Setbacks into Strategic Opportunities

Many successful startups were born from the ashes of previous failures, where lessons learned became the foundations for new strategies.

- **Analyzing Failure:** Understand what went wrong with past endeavors. Was it the business model, market timing, or something else? Each failure provides valuable insights that can lead to greater success in future efforts.

- **Pivoting:** Instead of heading back to the drawing board, successful entrepreneurs pivot their business strategies based on their experiences and market needs. This might mean altering a product, targeting a different audience, or overhauling a business model.

Case Studies of Resilient Entrepreneurs

Examining the journeys of those who have successfully navigated the entrepreneurial landscape can provide both inspiration and practical lessons:

- **Reid Hoffman:** Before founding LinkedIn, Hoffman was involved in SocialNet, a dating site that ultimately failed. He applied the lessons from this venture to create LinkedIn, focusing on professional networking.

- **Sara Blakely:** Founder of Spanx, Blakely turned an initial rejection from manufacturers into a motivation to develop her products. Her persistence led to a revolutionary line of shapewear that became a cultural phenomenon.

Innovative Thinking in Product Development

Entrepreneurship often involves developing new products or services. Innovative thinking is not just about creating something new but also about improving or repurposing existing products to meet unfulfilled needs.

- **Customer Feedback Loops:** Engaging with customers early and often helps in refining products and aligning them more closely with market demands.
- **Lean Startup Methodology:** This approach advocates for rapid prototyping, validated learning, and other strategies to efficiently use resources and quickly adapt to changing circumstances.

Funding the Venture

Securing funding is often one of the biggest challenges for startups. Entrepreneurs must be adept at navigating this landscape:

- **Bootstrap:** Funding the venture from personal savings or revenue from initial sales can be a way to maintain control over the business.

- **Venture Capital and Angel Investors:** For ventures with high growth potential, attracting investment from venture capital or angel investors can provide not just funding but also valuable mentorship and access to a broader network.

- **Crowdfunding:** Platforms like Kickstarter and Indiegogo allow entrepreneurs to raise funds directly from future customers, validating the product concept in the process.

Building a Support Network

No entrepreneur succeeds in isolation. Building a network of mentors, advisors, and fellow entrepreneurs can provide crucial support, advice, and resources. This network can be a lifeline during challenging times and a source of diverse perspectives that can enhance decision-making.

As we conclude this exploration of entrepreneurship, it is clear that the ability to transform setbacks into startups requires more than just a good idea—it demands a confluence of courage, creativity, and unwavering commitment. Armed with these insights and strategies, you are equipped to navigate the unpredictable yet rewarding waters of entrepreneurship. This chapter not only charts a course for emerging entrepreneurs but also cements the idea that with the right mindset, every setback can be reimagined as a stepping stone towards your next great venture.

Part IV: Developing a Winning Mindset

Chapter 10: Embracing Change and Uncertainty with Confidence

In a world where change is the only constant, the ability to adapt with confidence and resilience not only shapes individual careers but also defines the future of entire industries. This chapter explores how embracing change and managing uncertainty can become powerful tools for career development and personal growth.

Understanding the Nature of Change

Change in the professional landscape often comes without warning, requiring immediate and effective adaptation. Whether it's technological advancements, shifts in market demand, or global economic fluctuations, understanding the dynamics of change is crucial. It involves recognizing patterns, anticipating trends, and preparing mentally and practically for shifts that may alter career paths significantly.

Strategies for Adapting to Change

Adapting to change is not merely about survival but thriving. It requires a proactive approach:

- **Continuous Learning:** Stay ahead of industry trends by committing to lifelong learning. This could mean formal education, such as advanced degrees or certifications, or informal learning, like online courses and workshops.

- **Flexibility:** Develop a flexible mindset that welcomes change rather than fears it. This includes being open to new roles, industries, and even geographical relocations if they align with career growth opportunities.

- **Innovation:** Use changes as a springboard for innovation within your role or business. This could involve proposing new business processes, developing new products, or finding new markets for existing products.

Managing Uncertainty with Confidence

Uncertainty can be daunting, but handling it with confidence is a skill that can be developed through various practices:

- **Risk Management:** Identify potential risks in your career or industry and develop strategies to mitigate them. This could involve diversifying your skill set or creating a financial safety net.

- **Emotional Intelligence:** Develop your emotional intelligence to better handle stress, adapt to new situations, and communicate effectively under pressure.

- **Scenario Planning:** Regularly engage in scenario planning to prepare for various career outcomes. This helps reduce anxiety about the future and lays a clear path for navigating changes.

Real-Life Examples of Adapting to Change

Drawing inspiration from those who have successfully navigated significant changes can provide valuable lessons:

- **Tech Executives:** Leaders in technology companies often face rapid industry changes. For example, tech executives at companies like Adobe and Netflix have successfully pivoted their business models in response to new market conditions, shifting from traditional software licensing to cloud-based services and from DVD rentals to streaming, respectively.

- **Career Changers:** Consider the story of a marketing professional who transitioned to a data science career. By embracing the change necessitated by market demand, she undertook training in data analytics and machine learning, successfully pivoting her career path.

Building Resilience in the Face of Change

Resilience is perhaps the most critical attribute for managing change.

- **Develop a Growth Mindset:** View challenges as opportunities to grow and learn rather than obstacles.

- **Maintain a Strong Support Network:** Cultivate relationships with mentors, colleagues, and professionals who can provide guidance and support.

- **Stay Health-Conscious:** Manage stress through regular physical activity, adequate sleep, and healthy eating. A healthy body contributes to a resilient mind.

Conclusion

As this exploration into embracing change concludes, it becomes evident that navigating career shifts confidently isn't just about reacting to changes as they come but about continuously preparing for them. By fostering a mindset that views change as an integral part of growth, you equip yourself with the tools to not only anticipate shifts but to leverage them effectively. Armed with the strategies outlined in this chapter, you can turn the uncertainty of change into a definitive path toward career success and personal fulfillment, ultimately transforming potential upheavals into opportunities for advancement.

Chapter 11: The Psychology of Success: Grit and Growth Mindset

The journey toward career success is often less about external obstacles and more about internal battles. This chapter delves into the psychological underpinnings that distinguish the successful from the stagnant, focusing on the pivotal roles of grit and a growth mindset in navigating the complex pathways of professional life.

Defining Grit and Growth Mindset

Grit is the unwavering persistence and determination to continue despite difficulties, failures, or delays in success. It's about steadfastly pushing through challenges and maintaining an intense effort over time. Meanwhile, a growth mindset, a term coined by psychologist Carol Dweck, refers to the belief that one's abilities and intelligence can be developed through dedication, hard work, and learning. These two psychological pillars are often the bedrock of significant achievement and resilience.

The Role of Grit in Career Development

Individuals with high levels of grit are more likely to succeed in reaching their long-term goals. They view challenges as opportunities to grow rather than insurmountable obstacles.

- **Perseverance Over Perfection:** Gritty individuals do not seek a perfect journey; instead, they focus on progress, learning from setbacks and persistently moving forward.
- **Long-term Commitment:** They commit to their career goals for the long haul, showing sustained interest and effort over years, if not decades.

Cultivating a Growth Mindset in the Workplace

Adopting a growth mindset can transform your approach to work and development within a professional setting.

- **Embrace Challenges:** View challenges as chances to improve rather than threats to avoid. This perspective encourages stepping out of your comfort zone and fosters personal and professional growth.

- **Learn from Criticism:** Instead of taking feedback personally, see it as a valuable source of information that can help you improve, understanding that constructive criticism is a gift rather than a grievance.

- **Celebrate Others' Success:** Instead of feeling threatened by the success of others, consider their achievements as learning opportunities. This approach can broaden your understanding and expose you to new methods and ideas.

Integrating Grit and Growth Mindset into Career Strategy

To leverage these psychological strengths, integrate them into your career planning and daily work life.

- **Set Specific Goals:** Break your main objectives into smaller, manageable goals. This segmentation can make the process seem less daunting and provide clear next steps.

- **Develop Resilience:** Resilience can be built through experiences that push your limits. Seek out and engage in tasks that challenge you, whether through new projects, roles, or additional responsibilities.

- **Maintain Persistence:** Keep pushing forward, even when progress seems slow. Remember, success is a marathon, not a sprint.

Overcoming Psychological Barriers

Common psychological barriers such as fear of failure and impostor syndrome can derail even the most talented individuals.

- **Reframe Failure:** View failure as a stepping stone rather than a roadblock. Each failure is a lesson that brings you one step closer to your goals.
- **Address Impostor Syndrome:** Recognize your achievements and own them. Understand that feeling doubt does not mean lack of ability or success.

Practical Applications and Success Stories

This theoretical understanding is backed by numerous success stories from various fields.

- **Entrepreneurs:** Explore how startup founders use grit to overcome initial failures. For instance, consider the founders of Airbnb who persisted through numerous rejections and funding challenges.

- **Corporate Leaders:** Look at CEOs who have demonstrated a growth mindset by radically transforming business models or corporate cultures in response to changing market dynamics.

In conclusion, the journey toward mastering grit and adopting a growth mindset is both challenging and rewarding. By understanding and integrating these concepts into your personal and professional life, you prepare yourself not only to face the inevitable difficulties of career development but to thrive amidst them. This commitment to personal growth and perseverance is what ultimately paves the way for true and lasting success.

Chapter 12: Continuous Learning and Skill Development

In an era marked by rapid technological advancements and shifting economic landscapes, the commitment to continuous learning and skill development is not merely advantageous—it is essential. This chapter outlines the strategies and mindsets required to cultivate a lifelong learning ethos that can drive career success and personal growth in a perpetually changing world.

The Imperative of Lifelong Learning

The need for ongoing education and skill enhancement has never been more pronounced. As industries evolve and new technologies emerge, the half-life of skills is shrinking. This dynamic environment demands that professionals not only update their existing knowledge but also acquire new competencies to stay relevant and competitive.

- **Embracing a Learning Culture:** Cultivating an environment where learning is valued and promoted is crucial for personal and organizational success. This involves seeking out learning opportunities actively and encouraging others to do the same.

- **Learning Agility:** This key attribute involves the ability to quickly learn and apply new knowledge effectively. It is particularly valuable in today's fast-paced, ever-changing work scenarios.

Strategies for Effective Learning

Developing effective learning strategies is critical to ensure that the effort put into education translates into tangible career benefits.

- **Set Clear Learning Goals:** Identify specific skills and knowledge areas that align with your career objectives. Setting clear, measurable learning goals helps focus your efforts and provides motivation.

- **Utilize Diverse Learning Resources:** Take advantage of the myriad learning resources available today, from online courses and webinars to podcasts and eBooks. Platforms like Coursera, Udemy, LinkedIn Learning, and Khan Academy offer courses on a vast range of subjects.

- **Apply Learning to Practical Challenges:** The true test of knowledge is application. Try to apply what you learn to real-world situations, whether through projects at work, freelance assignments, or personal initiatives.

Building and Maintaining Technical Skills

In fields where technical skills are paramount, staying updated with the latest tools and technologies is essential.

- **Regular Training:** Engage in regular training sessions, workshops, and seminars. Many professional associations and organizations offer these for their members.

- **Certifications:** Obtaining industry-recognized certifications can validate your skills and make you a more attractive candidate for promotions or new job opportunities.

Developing Soft Skills

While technical skills may get your foot in the door, soft skills will open multiple doors in your career path.

- **Communication Skills:** Effective communication is crucial in nearly every profession. Developing this skill can dramatically improve your ability to work with teams, manage projects, and negotiate deals.
- **Leadership and Management Skills:** As you progress in your career, the ability to lead and manage others becomes essential. Leadership training can help you develop these skills before you assume a management role.

The Role of Mentorship in Learning

Mentorship can play a pivotal role in your learning journey. A mentor can provide guidance, share knowledge and experiences, and even help navigate career challenges.

- **Seeking Out Mentors:** Look for mentors who have the expertise and a career trajectory that aligns with your goals. This relationship should be mutually beneficial, where you can also offer value to your mentor.
- **Peer Learning:** Learning from peers, especially those who come from diverse backgrounds or have different skill sets, can provide fresh insights and new learning opportunities.

Creating a Personal Development Plan

A personal development plan is a detailed document that outlines your career goals, the skills you need to develop to achieve those goals, and the steps you will take to acquire those skills.

- **Regular Reviews:** Regularly review and update your development plan. This ensures that your learning objectives remain aligned with your evolving career goals.

Conclusion

As we conclude our exploration of continuous learning and skill development, it is clear that the cultivation of these habits is not just about personal or professional growth but about remaining adaptable and resilient in a world that values flexibility and preparedness. By embracing continuous learning, you not only future-proof your career but also enhance your ability to contribute meaningfully to your profession and society. This chapter has armed you with the strategies to integrate lifelong learning into your daily life, ensuring that every step you take is informed, intentional, and impactful.

Conclusion: Your Path to Triumph

Summing Up Key Insights and Strategies

Reflecting on the journey through "Triumph Over Trials: Harnessing Job Challenges into Career Milestones," it becomes clear that the path to career success is paved with more than just skill and opportunity; it is built on the resilience to face challenges, the wisdom to leverage one's experiences, and the foresight to continually adapt and grow. As we encapsulate the key insights and strategies discussed throughout this book, it's imperative to recognize that each concept interlinks to form a robust framework for navigating the complexities of modern employment landscapes.

Embracing Challenges as Opportunities

From the outset, the ability to view adversities as opportunities has stood as a fundamental theme. Whether turning economic downturns into career uplifts or navigating through layoffs to leadership roles, the stories and strategies highlighted have underscored the importance of a proactive approach. It's not merely about surviving in the face of adversity but thriving through innovation and adaptability.

Leveraging Modern Tools and Networks

The digital era has revolutionized how we approach job searching and career development. Mastery of digital platforms, from LinkedIn to various job portals, and the strategic use of social media for professional branding are no longer optional but essential. Networking emerges as an unseen lifeline, offering connections and opportunities that go beyond traditional job applications.

Cultivating a Resilient and Innovative Mindset

Chapters discussing the resilience of tech innovators and the creativity in the arts have shown that resilience is as much about emotional and mental strength as it is about practical skills. The stories of entrepreneurs turning setbacks into startups serve as powerful testaments to the strength of a resilient mindset combined with a flair for innovation.

Continuous Learning and Development

The commitment to continuous learning and skill development is perhaps the most crucial strategy for sustained career success. In a world where change is the only constant, staying relevant means staying educated. This is not just about formal education but also about engaging in lifelong learning through experiences, mentorships, and self-directed education.

Psychological Foundations of Success

Understanding and developing the psychological traits of grit and a growth mindset form the bedrock of enduring success. These traits enable individuals to persevere through challenges, learn from mistakes, and continually seek improvement, all of which are vital in a competitive job market.

Practical Applications and Real-World Relevance

The strategies discussed are not merely theoretical but are backed by practical applications and real-world examples. Each chapter provides actionable steps that individuals can take to apply these insights in their daily professional lives, ensuring that the lessons derived from this book are not just inspiring but also implementable.

Looking Forward

As we conclude, it's important to reflect on the notion that the journey of career development is perpetual. The landscape of work will continue to evolve, and so must we. By embracing the strategies laid out in this book, you equip yourself not just to respond to the demands of today's job market but to anticipate and thrive in the face of future changes.

This exploration, rich with practical advice and inspiring stories, is designed to be a companion in your ongoing career journey, offering guidance and wisdom that can help navigate through trials to triumph. Each chapter has built upon the last, creating a comprehensive guide that covers the essential aspects of modern career development, from harnessing digital tools to fostering personal growth through continuous learning.

As you move forward, keep these insights and strategies close at hand. Revisit them as you would consult a map on a long journey, allowing the wisdom contained within to guide you through new challenges and into new opportunities. Here's to your success, may it be as enduring as the principles laid out in this book, and may your career path be as triumphant as the stories of those who have walked before you.

Encouraging Personal Reflection and Action Steps

As we reach the culmination of "Triumph Over Trials: Harnessing Job Challenges into Career Milestones," it is essential not merely to have absorbed the information presented but to integrate these insights into actionable and personalized strategies. This closing section is dedicated to guiding you through a process of personal reflection and establishing clear, actionable steps based on the principles discussed throughout this book. By actively engaging in this process, you can transform insights into practical outcomes that propel your career forward.

Reflect on Your Career Path

Begin with a deep, introspective look at your current career trajectory:

- **Assess Your Current Position:** Where are you in your career right now? What are your strengths, and what areas need improvement?

- **Evaluate Challenges and Opportunities:** Reflect on the challenges you have faced so far. How have they shaped your career? What opportunities can you identify that may not have been apparent before?

- **Vision for the Future:** What does success look like to you in the long term? How do the insights from this book align with your career aspirations?

Set Specific, Measurable Goals

Using the SMART criteria (Specific, Measurable, Achievable, Relevant, Time-bound), set goals that are clear and attainable:

- **Short-term Goals:** What immediate steps can you take to begin applying what you've learned? This might involve enhancing your skill set, expanding your network, or updating your resume.

- **Long-term Goals:** Consider where you want to be in five to ten years. How do the principles of grit, growth mindset, and continuous learning play into achieving these goals?

Develop a Personalized Learning Plan

Continuous learning is vital for maintaining career momentum. Develop a plan that keeps you at the cutting edge of your industry:

- **Identify Learning Resources:** Based on your career goals, identify resources that can help you gain the necessary skills and knowledge. This could include books, courses, workshops, or conferences.

- **Schedule Regular Reviews:** Set a regular schedule to review and adjust your learning plan. This ensures that your learning objectives remain aligned with your evolving career goals.

Implementing a Networking Strategy

Networking has been underscored as a critical tool for career advancement. Plan how you will expand and engage with your network:

- **Identify Key Influencers:** Who are the key players in your field? How can you begin to engage with them? Perhaps start by connecting on LinkedIn and participating in relevant discussions.

- **Attend Industry Events:** Make a commitment to attend a certain number of industry events each year. These can be invaluable for meeting new people and staying informed about industry trends.

Embrace Change Proactively

Change is inevitable, so prepare to embrace it:

- **Stay Informed:** Keep up with industry news and trends. Subscribe to relevant publications, blogs, and podcasts.

- **Flexibility in Plans:** Be prepared to pivot your strategies as new information and opportunities arise. Flexibility can be a significant competitive advantage.

Maintain Physical and Mental Well-being

Success is not solely about professional achievements but also about maintaining your health and well-being:

- **Regular Exercise and Proper Nutrition:** Keep a regular exercise schedule and eat a balanced diet to maintain your physical health.

- **Mindfulness and Stress Management:** Practice mindfulness or meditation to manage stress. Remember, a clear mind leads to better performance.

Conclusion

Reflecting on your career and planning your future might seem daunting, but equipped with the strategies and insights from "Triumph Over Trials," you are now prepared to navigate the complexities of the modern job market with confidence and clarity. Each step you take, guided by the principles discussed, will build towards not just meeting but exceeding your career objectives. As you implement these action steps, keep in mind that every challenge you face is not just an obstacle but an opportunity to refine your skills, broaden your perspective, and advance your career. Now, step forward with confidence, knowing that you are well-equipped to turn your professional trials into triumphant milestones.

Appendices

Appendix A: Resources for Job Seekers

In navigating the complex terrain of modern employment, access to the right resources can significantly enhance your job search and career development efforts. This comprehensive guide provides an extensive array of tools and platforms designed to support you in various stages of your career journey. From identifying opportunities to enhancing your skills and networking effectively, the following resources are invaluable for any job seeker.

Online Job Boards and Career Websites

- **LinkedIn:** Beyond networking, LinkedIn offers job listings and insights into company cultures and potential connections. It's also a valuable platform for personal branding and establishing thought leadership in your field.

- **Indeed:** One of the most extensive job search engines, Indeed aggregates listings from thousands of websites, offering a vast range of opportunities across industries.

- **Glassdoor:** Known for company reviews and salary data, Glassdoor also offers job listings and valuable insights into company cultures and interview processes.

- **Monster:** A pioneer in the online recruitment industry, Monster remains a valuable resource for job listings and career advice.

Resume and Cover Letter Tools

- **Canva:** Offers a range of visually appealing resume templates that can help you stand out in your job application process.

- **Resume.io:** Provides tools to build professional resumes and cover letters that are tailored to specific job listings, enhancing your application's relevance and impact.

Interview Preparation

- **Big Interview:** An online system that combines training and practice to help you improve your interview technique and build your confidence.

- **Interview Cake:** Provides practice questions and coaching for tech industry interviews, particularly for software development positions.

Skill Development Platforms

- **Coursera:** Offers online courses from many of the world's top universities and companies, allowing you to learn at your own pace.

- **Udemy:** Features a vast selection of courses in a variety of subjects, from software development to personal development.

- **Pluralsight:** Focuses on tech skills, especially coding, IT operations, and cybersecurity.

- **Khan Academy:** Offers free courses on a wide range of subjects, including finance, mathematics, and computer programming.

Networking Opportunities

- **Meetup:** Allows you to find and join groups related to your industry interests, where you can meet like-minded professionals.

- **Eventbrite:** Provides a search tool for professional events, workshops, and seminars that can enhance your skills and expand your network.

- **Professional Associations:** Joining associations related to your field can provide networking opportunities, professional development resources, and industry insights.

Freelancing and Project Work

- **Upwork:** Connects freelancers with businesses looking for professionals to complete projects.

- **Freelancer:** Similar to Upwork, it offers a platform for freelancers to find project work across various disciplines.

- **Fiverr:** Allows creative professionals to offer their services and connect with potential clients on global projects.

Career Development and Advice

- **The Muse:** Offers a behind-the-scenes look at job opportunities, career advice, and access to coaches and courses.

- **CareerBuilder:** Provides not only job listings but also resources for writing resumes and preparing for interviews.

Maintaining Well-being and Work-Life Balance

- **Headspace:** Offers guided meditations and mindfulness practices to reduce stress and improve focus.

- **Calm:** Provides meditation techniques and sleep stories to help maintain mental health, crucial for job search and career resilience.

Conclusion

As this exploration of resources for job seekers concludes, remember that these tools are not just for finding a new job but for continuous professional development and personal growth. Integrating these resources into your daily routine can enhance your employability, keep you competitive in a dynamic job market, and support your journey through various career milestones. Whether you are starting out, seeking advancement, or pivoting to a new field, these tools provide a foundation for success. Let them guide and assist you as you navigate the path of your career, ensuring you are always moving forward, equipped with knowledge and supported by a network of opportunities.

Appendix B: Recommended Reading and Tools

In this journey through "Triumph Over Trials: Harnessing Job Challenges into Career Milestones," we've explored a myriad of strategies to navigate the complex landscape of modern employment. To further enhance your understanding and equip you with additional resources, this section outlines a curated list of books, publications, and tools that can expand your knowledge and skills. Each recommendation is selected for its potential to inspire, educate, and empower you in different facets of your career development.

Essential Books for Professional Growth

- **"Mindset: The New Psychology of Success" by Carol S. Dweck** - This book introduces the concept of the "growth mindset," a must-read for anyone looking to understand the psychological traits that promote personal and professional growth.

- **"Grit: The Power of Passion and Perseverance" by Angela Duckworth** - Duckworth explores the importance of grit as a predictor of success. This book is invaluable for understanding how determination and resilience can shape your career.

- **"Drive: The Surprising Truth About What Motivates Us" by Daniel H. Pink** - Pink provides profound insights into what motivates us, crucial for anyone aiming to find or reignite their passion for their career.

- **"How to Win Friends and Influence People" by Dale Carnegie** - A timeless guide to improving your interpersonal skills and building meaningful professional relationships.

- **"The 7 Habits of Highly Effective People" by Stephen R. Covey** - Covey's principles for personal and professional effectiveness can transform the way you approach your career and life challenges.

Advanced Publications for Industry Insights

- **Harvard Business Review** - Offers in-depth articles on leadership, organizational change, negotiation, strategy, operations, marketing, finance, and managing people.

- **The Economist** - Provides high-level insights into global business, finance, economics, and technology trends, helping you stay informed about the macro factors that influence various industries.

- **Industry Journals** - Depending on your field, specific journals like *Journal of Marketing* for marketers, *IEEE Spectrum* for engineers, or *Academy of Management Journal* for business management professionals can provide specialized knowledge.

Digital Tools for Skill Enhancement

- **LinkedIn Learning** - Offers video courses taught by industry experts in software, creative, and business skills.

- **Asana Academy** - Provides training on how to optimize project management skills, crucial for improving productivity and collaboration in any role.

- **Tableau Public** - Excellent for those interested in data visualization and business intelligence. Learning to use this tool can significantly enhance your analytical skills.

Podcasts for Continuous Learning

- **"How I Built This" with Guy Raz** - Raz interviews entrepreneurs, ideal for those seeking inspiration from the journeys of successful business founders.

- **"WorkLife" with Adam Grant** - Organizational psychologist Adam Grant explores workplace dynamics and how to make work not just tolerable but rewarding.

- **"The Tim Ferriss Show"** - Ferriss deconstructs world-class performers from eclectic areas, digging deep into the tools, tactics, and tricks that listeners can use.

Networking and Professional Development

- **Meetup** - Great for finding and joining local groups and events that can help you connect with like-minded professionals and expand your networking circle.

- **Shapr** - A networking app that connects you with professionals in your area who share your interests, helping you grow your professional network in a targeted way.

Conclusion

Armed with these resources, you are better prepared to tackle the challenges and opportunities that lie ahead in your professional journey. Whether through enhancing your understanding of psychological principles, improving your practical skills, or expanding your professional network, each tool and book is a step toward transforming job challenges into career milestones. Keep these resources handy as you navigate your path, allowing them to guide and enrich your career development continuously. Each resource is more than just a source of information—it's a companion on your journey to achieving and surpassing your career goals.

Appendix C: Glossary of Terms

In "Triumph Over Trials: Harnessing Job Challenges into Career Milestones," numerous terms are utilized to articulate the complex and nuanced world of career development and job market navigation. This glossary is intended to clarify these terms, providing you with a detailed understanding of the essential concepts discussed throughout the book. Each entry is crafted to enhance clarity and deepen your understanding of key principles that can influence your career trajectory.

Adaptability

- The ability to change or be changed to fit varied circumstances. In the context of career development, adaptability refers to the readiness and capacity to modify oneself or one's approach to professional challenges and changing job market conditions.

Career Resilience

- The capacity to navigate career setbacks, disruptions, or transitions effectively and to emerge from them stronger and more resourceful. It involves maintaining a positive and proactive attitude in the face of job-related adversities.

Continuous Learning

- The ongoing process of acquiring new knowledge and skills throughout one's career. Continuous learning is essential for keeping up-to-date with industry changes and maintaining competitiveness in the job market.

Digital Literacy

- The ability to find, evaluate, utilize, share, and create content using information technologies and the Internet. In today's job market, digital literacy is crucial for most professions as it enables individuals to engage effectively with digital platforms and tools.

Emotional Intelligence (EI)

- The capacity to be aware of, control, and express one's emotions, and to handle interpersonal relationships judiciously and empathetically. Emotional intelligence is a vital asset in managing professional relationships and navigating workplace challenges.

Grit

- A trait involving perseverance of effort combined with the passion for a particular long-term goal or end state. It helps individuals maintain their motivation over years despite failures, adversities, and plateaus in progress.

Growth Mindset

- The belief that one's fundamental abilities can be developed through dedication and hard work. This view creates a love of learning and a resilience that is essential for great accomplishment.

Networking

- The action or process of interacting with others to exchange information and develop professional or social contacts. In a career context, effective networking is often a critical element in job searching and career advancement.

Personal Branding

- The practice of marketing people and their careers as brands. Personal branding involves creating a distinct and memorable impression of oneself in the minds of others, particularly in professional contexts.

Resilience

- The capacity to recover quickly from difficulties; toughness. In professional terms, resilience refers to the ability to bounce back from career setbacks, adapt to change, and continue to pursue one's career objectives.

Skill Set

- A person's range of skills or competencies. Developing a diverse skill set is recommended for enhancing employability and adapting to various job roles or functions.

Virtual Interviewing

- The process of conducting job interviews online, typically using video conferencing tools. Virtual interviewing has become increasingly common in global and technologically advanced job markets.

Work-Life Balance

- The equilibrium between personal life and career work; the state of equal prioritization of the demands of one's career and the demands of one's personal life. Maintaining work-life balance is crucial for long-term job satisfaction and personal well-being.

Conclusion

This glossary serves as a tool to refine your understanding of the key terms used throughout this guide. By familiarizing yourself with these concepts, you can better navigate the complexities of the modern employment landscape, apply the strategies discussed in this book more effectively, and ultimately, achieve greater success in your career endeavors. Whether you are a recent graduate entering the job market, a mid-career professional seeking advancement, or an experienced executive aiming to pivot your career path, these terms lay the groundwork for a robust comprehension of the essential dynamics at play in your professional development.

About the Author

Morgan E. Blake is not merely a name but a beacon for those navigating the stormy waters of the modern job market. As an author and expert in employment and career development, Morgan has chosen to publish under this pseudonym not only to emphasize the universality and objectivity of the advice provided but also to allow the content to stand on its own merits, uncolored by personal history or bias.

Professional Background and Expertise

With a robust background in human resources, organizational behavior, and career counseling, Morgan brings a wealth of knowledge and practical experience to the field. This expertise is deeply rooted in a comprehensive understanding of the dynamics of employment trends and the evolving nature of workspaces across the globe. Morgan's professional journey has been marked by a commitment to helping individuals recognize and harness their potential, guiding them through transitions and challenges with strategic and empathetic insights.

Philosophy and Approach

Morgan's approach to career development is holistic and inclusive, advocating for a balance between achieving professional goals and maintaining personal well-being. This perspective is informed by years of research and hands-on experience, addressing the needs of a diverse workforce facing the unique challenges of the twenty-first century. The strategies Morgan advocates are not merely theoretical but are drawn from real-life contexts, making them both practical and adaptable to individual circumstances.

Contributions to the Field

Morgan E. Blake's contributions extend beyond individual counseling and advising. Through seminars, workshops, and published works, Morgan has influenced a broad audience, ranging from young professionals entering the workforce to seasoned executives seeking meaningful change in their career paths. Each interaction and piece of advice is geared towards empowering professionals to take proactive steps in shaping their careers.

"Triumph Over Trials: Harnessing Job Challenges into Career Milestones"

This latest work by Morgan E. Blake is a testament to a career spent in the trenches of career development. The book encapsulates the quintessence of overcoming professional adversity and transforming challenges into stepping stones for success. It synthesizes the insights gathered from a career dedicated to understanding the nuances of the job market, offering readers a practical guide to navigating their professional journeys.

Vision for the Future

Looking ahead, Morgan continues to focus on the pulse of employment trends, with a keen interest in how technological advancements and changing socio-economic factors influence career development. Committed to lifelong learning, Morgan remains at the forefront of educational innovation, ensuring that the guidance provided remains relevant and impactful.

Engagement with Readers

Morgan values the connection with readers, considering their feedback and success stories as the true measure of the work's value. Engaging actively through various online platforms and public speaking engagements, Morgan fosters a community of motivated individuals who are eager to learn, grow, and succeed.

Conclusion

In conclusion, Morgan E. Blake represents a source of reliability and inspiration in the field of career guidance. As you turn the pages of "Triumph Over Trials," you engage not just with the insights of a seasoned expert but with a mentor who is genuinely invested in your journey to career success. With each chapter, Morgan invites you to explore, learn, and ultimately, triumph in your own professional life.

Summary

Introduction: The Journey from Challenge to Triumph............ 3

    Setting the Stage: What It Means to Triumph in Today's Job Market.. 3

    Overview of Success Stories to be Explored........................... 6

Part I: Recognizing Opportunities in Adversity 10

    Chapter 1: Turning Economic Downturns into Career Uplifts.. 10

        Strategies for Career Pivoting 11

        Real-Life Examples of Career Transformation........... 12

        Leveraging Economic Indicators 12

        Staying Motivated and Resilient................................. 12

        Conclusion of the Chapter.. 13

    Chapter 2: Navigating Career Transitions: From Layoffs to Leadership 14

        Understanding the Psychological Impact of Layoffs ... 14

        Strategic Steps to Leadership After a Layoff................ 14

        Real-Life Success Stories 16

        Leveraging Leadership Skills....................................... 16

        Embracing a Forward-Thinking Mindset 17

    Chapter 3: Innovating Job Search Strategies in the Digital Era.. 18

        The Shift to Digital Platforms 18

        Optimizing Your Digital Presence............................... 18

        Leveraging Social Media for Job Searching 19

Advanced Tools and Analytics 20
Networking in the Digital Age 20
Case Studies: Success Through Innovation 21
Embracing a Culture of Continuous Learning 21
Part II: Strategic Tools for Modern Job Hunting 23
Chapter 4: Leveraging Social Media for Career Advancement 23
Building a Professional Online Persona 23
Engaging with Industry Leaders and Peers 24
Using Social Media to Research Companies 25
Crafting a Personal Brand 26
Navigating Challenges and Pitfalls 26
Harnessing the Full Spectrum of Social Media Tools . 27
Chapter 5: Networking: The Unseen Lifeline of Successful Careers 28
The Essence of Networking 28
Strategies for Effective Networking 29
Digital Networking and Its Impact 29
Leveraging Networks for Career Transitions 30
The Role of Networking in Job Searches 30
Networking as a Lifelong Process 31
Building a Diverse and Inclusive Network 31
Chapter 6: Mastering Remote Job Interviews and Virtual Hiring Processes 32
Understanding the Virtual Interview Landscape 32
Preparing for the Virtual Interview 33

Enhancing Communication Skills for Virtual Formats 33

Anticipating and Answering Interview Questions 34

Following Up Post-Interview 35

Common Pitfalls to Avoid 35

Embracing the Digital Interview Era 36

Part III: Case Studies of Success 37

Chapter 7: The Career Resilience of Tech Innovators 37

Navigating the Fast-Paced Tech Landscape 37

Case Studies of Resilient Tech Leaders 38

Building Resilience in Tech Careers 38

The Role of Mentorship and Community 39

Leveraging Setbacks as Stepping Stones 40

Embracing Change and Uncertainty 40

Chapter 8: Creative Industries: Adapting and Thriving Against the Odds 41

The Ever-Evolving Creative Landscape 41

Technological Disruption and Opportunity 42

Navigating Financial Instability 43

Building a Personal Brand 43

Case Studies of Creative Resilience 44

Adapting to Market Needs 44

The Importance of Community and Collaboration 45

Chapter 9: Entrepreneurs and the Art of Turning Setbacks into Start-ups 45

Understanding the Entrepreneurial Mindset 46

Turning Setbacks into Strategic Opportunities 47

Case Studies of Resilient Entrepreneurs 47

Innovative Thinking in Product Development 48

Funding the Venture 48

Building a Support Network 49

Part IV: Developing a Winning Mindset 51

Chapter 10: Embracing Change and Uncertainty with Confidence 51

Understanding the Nature of Change 51

Strategies for Adapting to Change 52

Managing Uncertainty with Confidence 52

Real-Life Examples of Adapting to Change 53

Building Resilience in the Face of Change 54

Conclusion 54

Chapter 11: The Psychology of Success: Grit and Growth Mindset 55

Defining Grit and Growth Mindset 55

The Role of Grit in Career Development 56

Cultivating a Growth Mindset in the Workplace 56

Integrating Grit and Growth Mindset into Career Strategy 57

Overcoming Psychological Barriers 58

Practical Applications and Success Stories 58

Chapter 12: Continuous Learning and Skill Development 59

The Imperative of Lifelong Learning 60

Strategies for Effective Learning 60

- Building and Maintaining Technical Skills ... 61
- Developing Soft Skills ... 62
- The Role of Mentorship in Learning ... 62
- Creating a Personal Development Plan ... 63
- Conclusion ... 63

Conclusion: Your Path to Triumph ... 65
- Summing Up Key Insights and Strategies ... 65
  - Embracing Challenges as Opportunities ... 65
  - Leveraging Modern Tools and Networks ... 66
  - Cultivating a Resilient and Innovative Mindset ... 66
  - Continuous Learning and Development ... 66
  - Psychological Foundations of Success ... 67
  - Practical Applications and Real-World Relevance ... 67
  - Looking Forward ... 67
- Encouraging Personal Reflection and Action Steps ... 68
  - Reflect on Your Career Path ... 69
  - Set Specific, Measurable Goals ... 70
  - Develop a Personalized Learning Plan ... 70
  - Implementing a Networking Strategy ... 71
  - Embrace Change Proactively ... 71
  - Maintain Physical and Mental Well-being ... 72
  - Conclusion ... 72

Appendices ... 74
- Appendix A: Resources for Job Seekers ... 74
  - Online Job Boards and Career Websites ... 74
  - Resume and Cover Letter Tools ... 75

Interview Preparation 75
 Skill Development Platforms 76
 Networking Opportunities 76
 Freelancing and Project Work 77
 Career Development and Advice 77
 Maintaining Well-being and Work-Life Balance 77
 Conclusion 78
Appendix B: Recommended Reading and Tools 78
 Essential Books for Professional Growth 79
 Advanced Publications for Industry Insights 80
 Digital Tools for Skill Enhancement 81
 Podcasts for Continuous Learning 81
 Networking and Professional Development 82
 Conclusion 82
Appendix C: Glossary of Terms 83
 Adaptability 83
 Career Resilience 83
 Continuous Learning 84
 Digital Literacy 84
 Emotional Intelligence (EI) 84
 Grit 85
 Growth Mindset 85
 Networking 85
 Personal Branding 85
 Resilience 86
 Skill Set 86

- Virtual Interviewing 86
- Work-Life Balance 87
- Conclusion 87

About the Author 88
- Professional Background and Expertise............................88
- Philosophy and Approach..88
- Contributions to the Field...89
- "Triumph Over Trials: Harnessing Job Challenges into Career Milestones"...89
  - Vision for the Future 90
  - Engagement with Readers..90
  - Conclusion 90

www.ingramcontent.com/pod-product-compliance
Lightning Source LLC
Chambersburg PA
CBHW050118230526
45470CB00004B/1890